Relief Society
WHERE IT ALL BEGAN

Text by
SUSAN EASTON BLACK

Art by
LIZ LEMON SWINDLE

NAUVOO GREW, with magic rapidity, from a few rude homes to a magnificent city," penned journalist Harvey Cluff. Yet, not every resident of Nauvoo prospered in the 1840s. "It is a hard place for poor people that have no money to get a living," wrote Sally Randall. "There are so many poor . . . they can hardly get enough to be comfortable." One such man was Luman Shurtliff, a laborer in the stone quarries. "We labored ten hours a day, and got something to take to our families for supper and breakfast. Many times we got nothing," wrote Shurtliff.

Sarah Kimball witnessed the struggles of faithful stone cutters like Luman Shurtliff. She wanted to help, as did her seamstress Miss Cook. "I told [Miss Cook] I would furnish material if she would make some shirts for the workman," wrote Sarah. These two women combined their talents to assist the poor of Nauvoo.

Near neighbors saw their charitable kindness and expressed a desire to also help. Sarah recalled, "We decided to . . . form a ladies society" to help the poor. "The neighboring sisters met in my parlor and organized" on March 4, 1842. To be organized like other benevolent societies in the midwestern states required a constitution and an election of officers. Sarah asked Eliza R. Snow to create the constitution and bylaws of the society before elections were held.

Eliza did her best on the proposed documents and showed the results of her efforts to the Prophet Joseph Smith. He lauded her accomplishments and stated that the constitution and by-laws were "the best he had ever seen." But he wanted to "provide something better for [the women of Nauvoo] than a written constitution. I will organize the women under the priesthood after the pattern of the priesthood."

On Thursday, March 17, 1842, twenty women from the ages of a teenager to a widow in her fifties, crowded into the upper story of the Prophet's store on Water Street in Nauvoo. There thirty-eight year old Emma Smith was elected to be the first president of The Female Relief Society of Nauvoo and as such "to look to the wants of the needy and be a pattern of virtue and possess all the qualifications necessary for her to stand and preside and dignify her office."

The Prophet admonished members of the newly constituted society to "not injure the character of anyone, . . . hold all character sacred." Eliza R. Snow concurred by adding, "As daughters of Zion, we should set an example for all the world." Emma then exclaimed, "We are going to do something extra ordinary. When a boat is stuck on the rapids, with a multitude of Mormons on board we shall consider that a loud call for relief. We expect extraordinary occasions and pressing calls."

Impressed by the sincerity of their expressions, the Prophet arose and declared, "All I shall have to give to the poor, I will give to the society." He then gave a $5 dollar gold piece. His example led others to likewise contribute. John Taylor, noting the abundant generosity,

THREE

stated, "His prayer [was] that the blessing of God and of heaven may rest on this institution henceforth."

THE GREAT WORK of the Relief Society had begun. A vision of women reaching out and helping others soon extended to every neighborhood in Nauvoo. Although a Sister Merrick is credited with being the first recipient of the Society's compassion, she soon became one of many whose burdens were lifted. The joy of receiver and giver seemed unbounded. Those with means gave freely and those without means contributed jewelry and clothing, talents and skills--all gifts were welcome. Most women believed, "Nothing was more laudable than feeding the hungry, and clothing the naked."

Witnessing their many unselfish acts in the name of the Relief Society was the Prophet's mother, Lucy Mack Smith. She stated, "This institution is a good one. We must cherish one another, watch over one another, comfort one another and gain instruction that we may all sit down in heaven together. . . . And then she wept." Why such charity? Perhaps Sarah Cleveland explained it best, "We have entered into this work in the name of the Lord. Let us boldly go forward." With boldness Sarah Cleveland mentioned a widow and child needed a friend and home. One unhesitating woman responded to the immediacy of the situation by taking the widow and child into her own home. Whether the gift of service was a home, a hearth, a quilt cover, gown, or wristlets the gift was extended with love and embraced with gratitude.

As the Prophet Joseph Smith observed the outpouring of love, he acknowledged, "It is natural for females to have feelings of charity. You are now placed in a situation where you can act according to those sympathies which God has planted in your bosoms. If you live up to your privileges the angels cannot be restrained from being your associates."

"This society shall have power to command queens in their midst," he continued. "Queens of the earth shall come and pay their respects to this society. They shall come with their millions and shall contribute of their abundance for the relief of the poor. If you will be pure, nothing can hinder."

Joseph admonished the sisters, "Don't be limited in your views with regard to your neighbor's virtues, but be limited towards your own virtues. You must enlarge your soul towards others. . . . Let this society teach how to act towards husbands, to treat them with mildness and affection. When a man is born down with trouble, when he is perplexed, if he can meet a smile, not an argument, if he can meet mildness, it will calm down his soul and soothe his feelings. . . . If one member suffer, all feel it. By union of feeling we obtain power with God."

Joseph Smith then said, "I now turn the key to you in the name of God and this society shall rejoice and knowledge and intelligence shall flow down from this time. This is the beginning of better days to this society."

And better days did follow. The women of Nauvoo poured in "oil and wine to the wounded heart of the distressed; they dry[ed] up the tears of the orphan and made the widow's heart to rejoice." Indeed, generosity and gratitude were reported in every neighborhood of Nauvoo. One recipient, Ellen Douglas, an immigrant from England, being too ill to mend her children's clothes reported that a Relief Society sister "fetched me such a present as I never received before from no place in the world. I suppose the things they sent were as much as 30 schillings." The whispering of the spirit led sisters Mary Fielding Smith and Mercy Thompson to encourage women "to subscribe 1 cent per week for the purpose of buying glass and nails for the temple." In this manner they raised over $1000 for the Nauvoo Temple. And so the kindness extended from one to another became like a tide of rushing waters bursting forth upon the earth in one great continuum.

The Relief Society of The Church of Jesus Christ of Latter-day Saints continues to extend compassion to the world's down-trodden. From Africa to the Orient and from Europe to South America the less fortunate are made glad by the thoughtful kindness of women in this society. As recipients of their kindness, we give thanks.

REFERENCES   Smith, *History of the Church* 3:375; 4:567, 4:605-06, 6:549; Roberts, *Comprehensive History of the Church* 2:9; Harvey Cluff Autobiography, typescript, BYU-S, 4-5; Derr, et. al, *Woman of Covenant*, 1-20; Luman Shurtliff Autobiography, typescript, BYU-S, 52-53; Smith and Thomas, *When the Key was Turned*, p. 17; Minutes of the Relief Society, March 17, 1842; March 24, 1842; April 28, 1842; May 26, 1842.

©2001 Susan Easton Black and Liz Lemon Swindle

All rights reserved. No part of this book may be reproduced in any form or by any means without permission in writing from the publisher, Millennial Press Inc. This work is not an official publication of The Church of Jesus Christ of Latter-day Saints. The views expressed herein are the responsibility of the author and do not necessarily represent the position of the Church or of Millennial Press Inc.

Design: Scott Eggers

Millenial Press, Inc.
P.O. Box 1741
Orem, Utah 84059

801-434-7478 phone
www.millennialpress.com

ISBN 0-9660231-5-3 $2.49

Printed in the United States of America

10   9   8   7   6   5   4